Joanna MacGregor's PianoWorld

VERY FIRST ADVENTURES IN PIANO PLAYING

A Christmas Story

by Joanna MacGregor

with illustrations by Stik

For more information about PianoWorld and Joanna MacGregor, contact: fabermusic.com/pianoworld and soundcircus.com

© 2002 by Faber Music Ltd
First published in 2002 by Faber Music Ltd
3 Queen Square London WC1N 3AU
Music arrangements by Joanna MacGregor
Music processed by Jeanne Fisher
Printed in England by Caligraving Ltd
ISBN 0-571-51988-1

To buy Faber Music publications or to find out about the full range of titles available please contact your local music retailer or Faber Music sales enquiries:

Faber Music Limited, Burnt Mill, Elizabeth Way, Harlow, CM20 2HX England
Tel: +44 (0)1279 82 89 82   Fax: +44 (0)1279 82 89 83
sales@fabermusic.com   fabermusic.com

Grumper didn't like Christmas. All that rushing around buying presents, going to parties, decorating the Christmas tree. What a lot of bother! And what made it worse, he'd fallen out with Ned, and Ned had run away.

Tremblin' Christmas Blues

Joanna MacGregor

Tremolo: alternate between two notes in each hand as quickly as possible! Try holding down the right pedal in the tremolo bars.

optional accompaniment

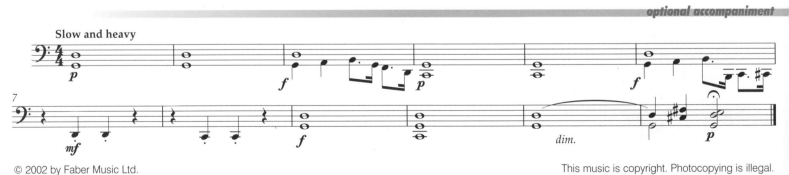

4 Grumper

But Grumper's grump was suddenly disturbed – he couldn't believe his ears!
In the next room the Scherzo Sisters were practising for their carol concert ...

alt.country Jingle Bells

James Pierpont

Jin - gle bells, jin - gle bells, jin - gle all the way! Oh what fun it
is to ride on a one horse o - pen sleigh. Oh! one horse o - pen sleigh!

sleigh bells—
As many as you like!

*the little note is a 'grace note': play as quickly as possible before the main note.

optional accompaniment

sim.

As many times as your pupil likes!

'Well, there's one good thing,' said Grumper. 'At least I haven't seen snow in PianoWorld for years and years. There's nothing worse than having a freezing nose and cold paws'. Whoosh! The Scherzo Sisters were suddenly next to him, shouting: 'It's Christmas Eve, and we've got to go shopping! We're meeting Crash Harry at the PianoWorld Megastore.'

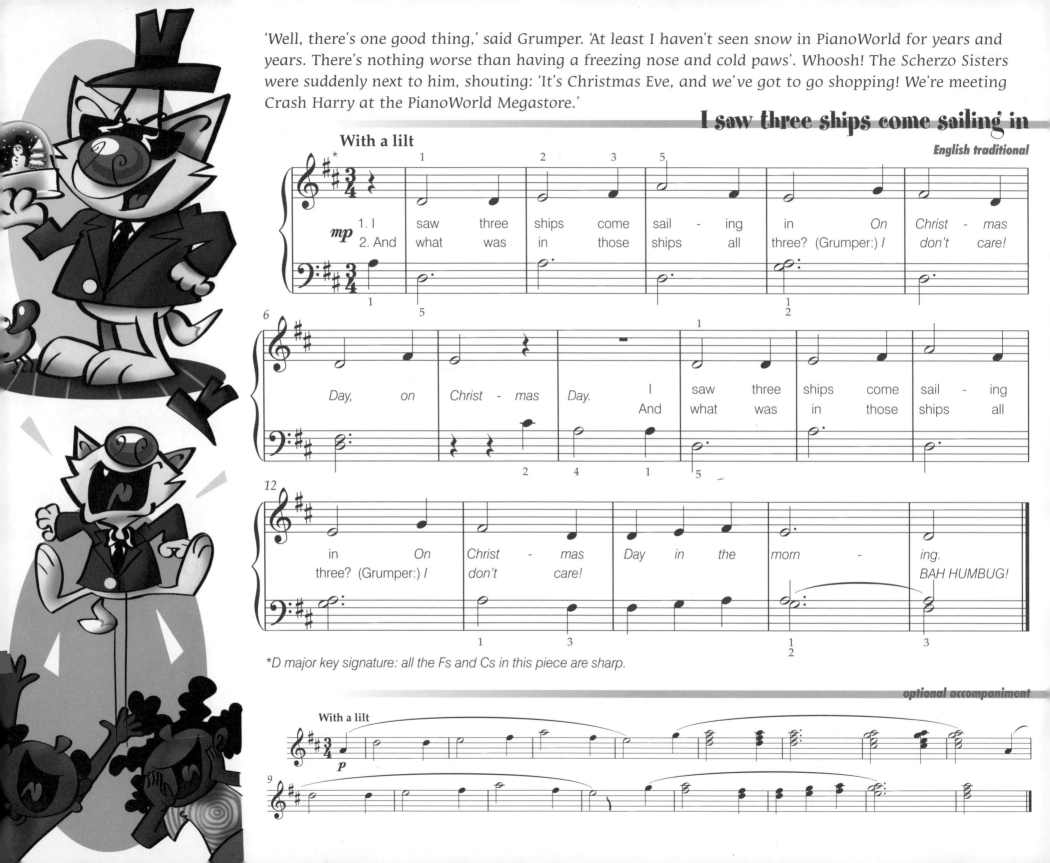

I saw three ships come sailing in

English traditional

*D major key signature: all the Fs and Cs in this piece are sharp.

optional accompaniment

At the PianoWorld shopping arcade, the Scherzo Sisters gasped but Grumper groaned.
Twinkling fairy lights criss-crossed the roof, winking down at them.
Christmas trees lined the pathway, all decorated with tinsel and holly.

Deck the hall with boughs of holly

Welsh traditional

But then they saw a sleeping bag underneath one of the Christmas trees, with a sign: 'Cold and Hungry'. 'Spare some change', said a small voice. 'Oh dear. He's not going to have a happy Christmas,' the Scherzo Sisters said to each other.

Lonely Christmas

Joanna MacGregor

The *Scherzo Sisters* – and even Grumper – thought how lucky they were to live in a warm home with their friends. They remembered a song that used to be sung to them when they were very small and were unhappy.

We will rock you

Czech carol

Very gentle

mp Lit - tle Je - sus, sweet - ly__ sleep, do not__ stir; we will__ lend a__

coat of__ fur. We will rock you, rock you, rock you. See the fur to keep you__ warm,

snug - ly__ round your__ ti - ny__ form. *p* (*falling asleep*) **rit.** *dim.* *pp*

Text: Percy Dearmer © 1928 Oxford University Press. Used by permission.

optional accompaniment

Very gentle

pp lots of pedal

rit. *p* *dim.* *pp*

'His voice sounds familiar,' said the Scherzo Sisters. But Grumper, who was worried about what Crash Harry could be getting up to, hurried them towards the store. Just outside was the famous magical Christmas tree in which all sorts of extraordinary animals lived – kangaphants and tortiberts, ridditusks and gillipots. And under the branches of the tree, there was an enormous Santa's grotto, covered in snow and long, glistening icicles. 'Ho Ho Ho!' they heard.

Ho Ho Ho Song

Joanna MacGregor

At the PianoWorld shopping arcade, the Scherzo Sisters gasped but Grumper groaned.
Twinkling fairy lights criss-crossed the roof, winking down at them.
Christmas trees lined the pathway, all decorated with tinsel and holly.

Deck the hall with boughs of holly

Welsh traditional

But then they saw a sleeping bag underneath one of the Christmas trees, with a sign: 'Cold and Hungry'.
'Spare some change', said a small voice. 'Oh dear. He's not going to have a happy Christmas,'
the Scherzo Sisters said to each other.

Lonely Christmas

Joanna MacGregor

The *Scherzo Sisters* – and even Grumper – thought how lucky they were to live in a warm home with their friends. They remembered a song that used to be sung to them when they were very small and were unhappy.

We will rock you

Czech carol

Text: Percy Dearmer © 1928 Oxford University Press. Used by permission.

'His voice sounds familiar,' said the Scherzo Sisters. But Grumper, who was worried about what Crash Harry could be getting up to, hurried them towards the store. Just outside was the famous magical Christmas tree in which all sorts of extraordinary animals lived – kangaphants and tortiberts, ridditusks and gillipots. And under the branches of the tree, there was an enormous Santa's grotto, covered in snow and long, glistening icicles. 'Ho Ho Ho!' they heard.

Ho Ho Ho Song

Joanna MacGregor

Then they *saw* something that looked like a beach, and a sandcastle. 'G'day!', said a boy in green shorts and a Santa hat, clutching a surf board, 'Do you want something from the Bar-B?' An Australian Christmas!

The 12 days of Christmas/12 days down under

Sing the traditional words or the new Australian ones!

English traditional

Con brio

1. On the first day of Christ-mas my true love gave to me
{ a par-tridge__ in a pear
a bur-ger__ on a Bar -

tree.
- B.

2-3. On the se-cond day of Christ-mas my true love gave to me
third

repeat as necessary

{ *2 tur - tle doves
2 *Nike train-ers*
{ 3 French__ hens
3 *brand new bikes*
and a { par - tridge__ in a pear tree.
bur - ger__ on a Bar - B.

D. %

Fourth day: 4 calling birds / *4 rugby balls*
Fifth day: 5 gold rings / *5 Barbie dolls*
Sixth day: 6 geese a-laying / *6 kookaburras*
Seventh day: 7 swans a-swimming / *7 cricket bats*
Eighth day: 8 maids a-milking / *8 didgeridoos*

Ninth day: 9 ladies dancing / *9 swimming pools*
Tenth day: 10 lords a-leaping / *10 kangaroos*
Eleventh day: 11 pipers piping / *11 koala bears*
Twelfth day: 12 drummers drumming / *12 surfing boards*

*Start with the new number and present, and then all the others, counting downwards!

The three friends were just about to tuck into one of Bruce's Brilliant Burgers, when … CRASH!!!
Crash Harry! The magical Christmas tree had toppled side ways and was lying on the ground –
Harry's head could be seen peeping through the tree's branches. 'What happened?' Grumper shouted
at Crash Harry. 'Well, I saw a bag of sweets in the top branches, and I thought they needed eating.
I started to climb the tree and it fell over and landed on the Christmas Crib on top of the little donkey
and …' 'Oh for goodness sake!' grumbled Grumper.

The donkey carol

Eric Boswell

'Excuse me', said the Scherzo Sisters impatiently, 'the shop shuts in 45 minutes, and we haven't bought any presents yet! We'd better get on with it.' The crowds were terrible – everyone pushing and shoving, grabbing anything off the shelves, with queues that went up the stairs and onto the next floor.

Shopping rage

Joanna MacGregor

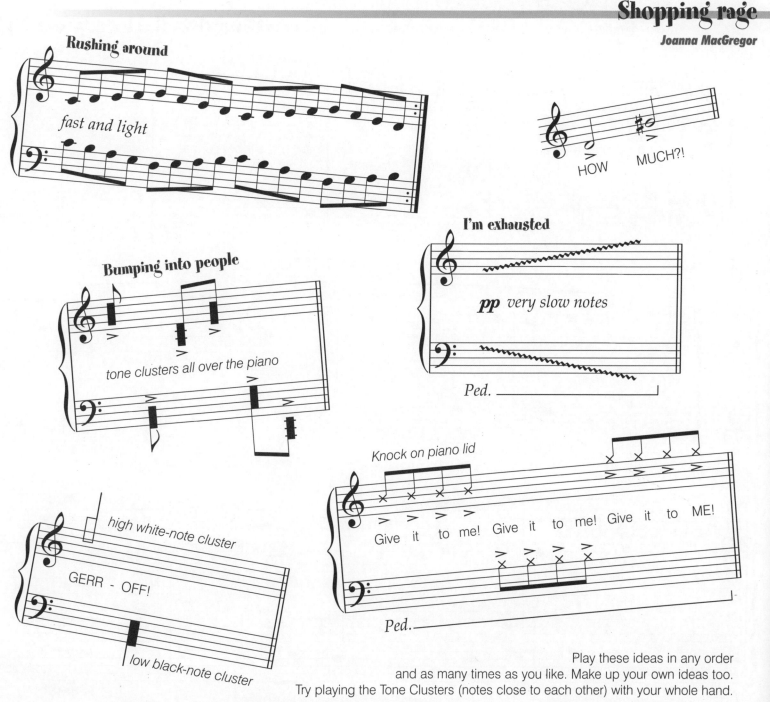

Play these ideas in any order
and as many times as you like. Make up your own ideas too.
Try playing the Tone Clusters (notes close to each other) with your whole hand.

Phew! They'd done it. Clutching their bags stuffed full with presents, the Scherzo Sisters and Crash Harry stumbled out of the store. Grumper hadn't bought anything. He'd stuffed cotton wool in his ears – he was fed up with Christmas Carols Muzak, particularly the jolly ones.

Ding dong! Merrily on high

Thoinot Arbeau

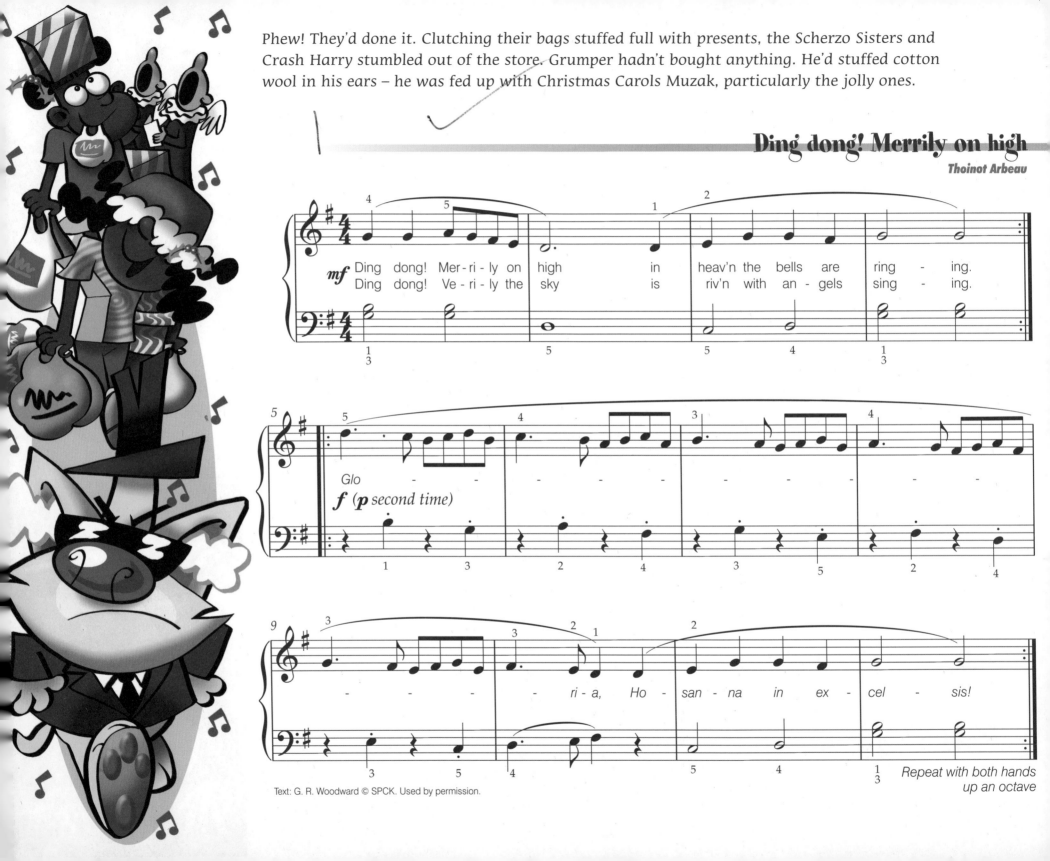

mf Ding dong! Mer‑ri‑ly on high in heav'n the bells are ring – ing.
Ding dong! Ve‑ri‑ly the sky is riv'n with an‑gels sing – ing.

Glo
f (*p* second time)

Glo – – – – – – – – – – – – ri‑a, Ho‑ san‑na in ex‑ cel – sis!

Repeat with both hands up an octave

Then they *saw* something that looked like a beach, and a sandcastle. 'G'day!', said a boy in green shorts and a Santa hat, clutching a surf board, 'Do you want something from the Bar-B?' An Australian Christmas!

The 12 days of Christmas/12 days down under

Sing the traditional words or the new Australian ones!

English traditional

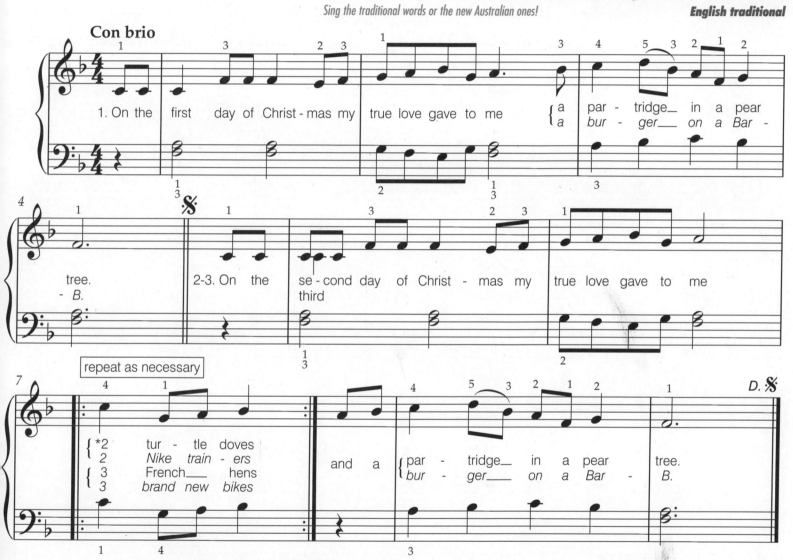

Con brio

1. On the first day of Christ - mas my true love gave to me { a par - tridge__ in a pear { a bur - ger__ on a Bar -

tree.
- B.

2-3. On the se - cond day of Christ - mas my true love gave to me
third

repeat as necessary

{ *2 tur - tle doves
2 *Nike train - ers*
3 French__ hens
3 *brand new bikes*

and a { par - tridge__ in a pear tree.
{ bur - ger__ on a Bar - B.

D. %

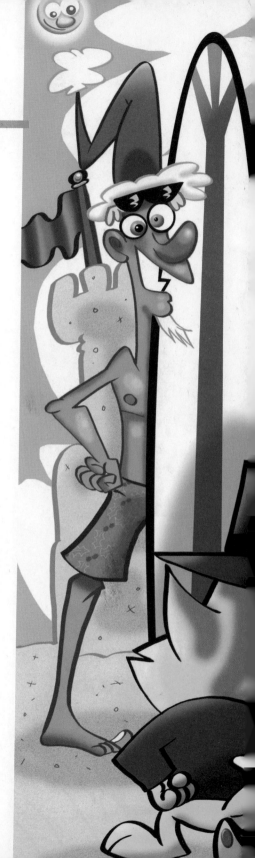

Fourth day: 4 calling birds / *4 rugby balls*
Fifth day: 5 gold rings / *5 Barbie dolls*
Sixth day: 6 geese a-laying / *6 kookaburras*
Seventh day: 7 swans a-swimming / *7 cricket bats*
Eighth day: 8 maids a-milking / *8 didgeridoos*

Ninth day: 9 ladies dancing / *9 swimming pools*
Tenth day: 10 lords a-leaping / *10 kangaroos*
Eleventh day: 11 pipers piping / *11 koala bears*
Twelfth day: 12 drummers drumming / *12 surfing boards*

*Start with the new number and present, and then all the others, counting downwards!

The three friends were just about to tuck into one of Bruce's Brilliant Burgers, when ... CRASH!!!
Crash Harry! The magical Christmas tree had toppled side ways and was lying on the ground –
Harry's head could be seen peeping through the tree's branches. 'What happened?' Grumper shouted
at Crash Harry. 'Well, I saw a bag of sweets in the top branches, and I thought they needed eating.
I started to climb the tree and it fell over and landed on the Christmas Crib on top of the little donkey
and ...' 'Oh for goodness sake!' grumbled Grumper.

The donkey carol

Eric Boswell

'Excuse me', said the Scherzo Sisters impatiently, 'the shop shuts in 45 minutes, and we haven't bought any presents yet! We'd better get on with it.' The crowds were terrible – everyone pushing and shoving, grabbing anything off the shelves, with queues that went up the stairs and onto the next floor.

Shopping rage

Joanna MacGregor

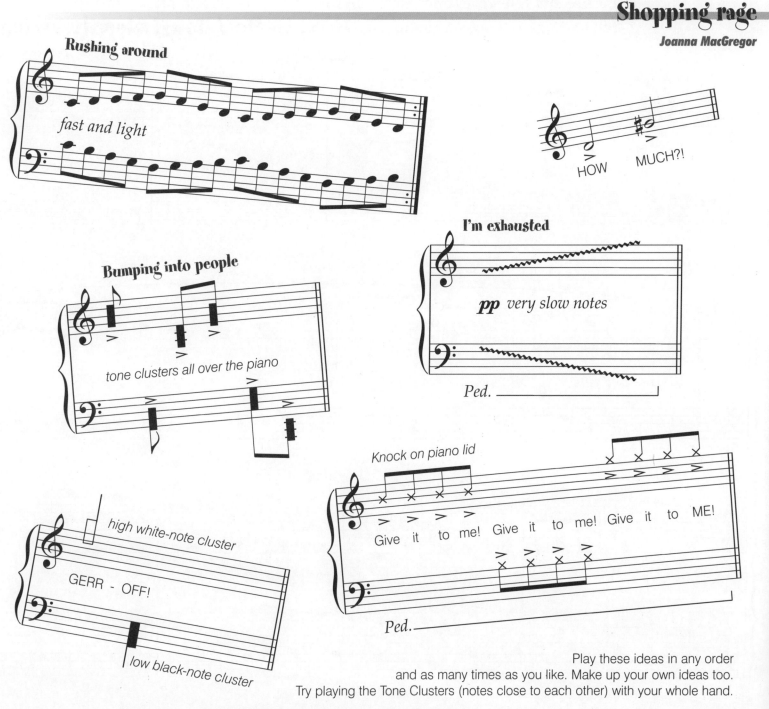

Play these ideas in any order
and as many times as you like. Make up your own ideas too.
Try playing the Tone Clusters (notes close to each other) with your whole hand.

Phew! They'd done it. Clutching their bags stuffed full with presents, the *Scherzo Sisters* and *Crash Harry* stumbled out of the store. Grumper hadn't bought anything. He'd stuffed cotton wool in his ears – he was fed up with Christmas Carols Muzak, particularly the jolly ones.

Ding dong! Merrily on high

Thoinot Arbeau

Ding dong! Mer - ri - ly on high in heav'n the bells are ring - ing.
Ding dong! Ve - ri - ly the sky is riv'n with an - gels sing - ing.

Glo - - - - - - - - -

- - - - ri - a, Ho - san - na in ex - cel - sis!

Repeat with both hands up an octave

On the way home, they walked past the sleeping bag with the sign 'Cold and Hungry'. 'Who could it be?' asked the Scherzo Sisters: they were thinking about leaving a present. 'Oh come along', miaowed Grumper. 'Let's get back. I could do with a nap, and I suppose you'll want to be decorating that stupid tree.' At home, Grumper fell asleep in front of the fire, but heard a sad tune in his head …

The little fir tree

Swedish folktune

optional accompaniment

Grumper was half asleep. Then he seemed to see a ghost who led him out of the window and back to the shopping mall … He looked and saw himself in a sleeping bag outside the shopping mall, lonely and hungry. He was singing a carol, hoping that people would give him a little money, but they were ignoring him, and hurrying past with bags full of food and presents.

Try playing some 'ghosty' music here: put the pedal down and play very soft notes.

Away in a manger

William J Kirkpatrick

Grumper was wide awake. 'Was that a dream, or did I really meet a ghost?' He sprang up and, wrapping his scarf around his neck, bounded out of the house towards the arcade. Under the light of the moon, the fairy lights were still twinkling. He found the little figure in a sleeping bag. 'Please don't sit there all alone. It's Christmas tomorrow – come back to our house. There's plenty to go around.' The little figure stood up. 'Why thank you, Grumper,' he said. It was Ned! Grumper felt something soft and white fall upon his nose. 'Look!' said Ned, 'it's snowing!'

Christmas Bells

Joanna MacGregor

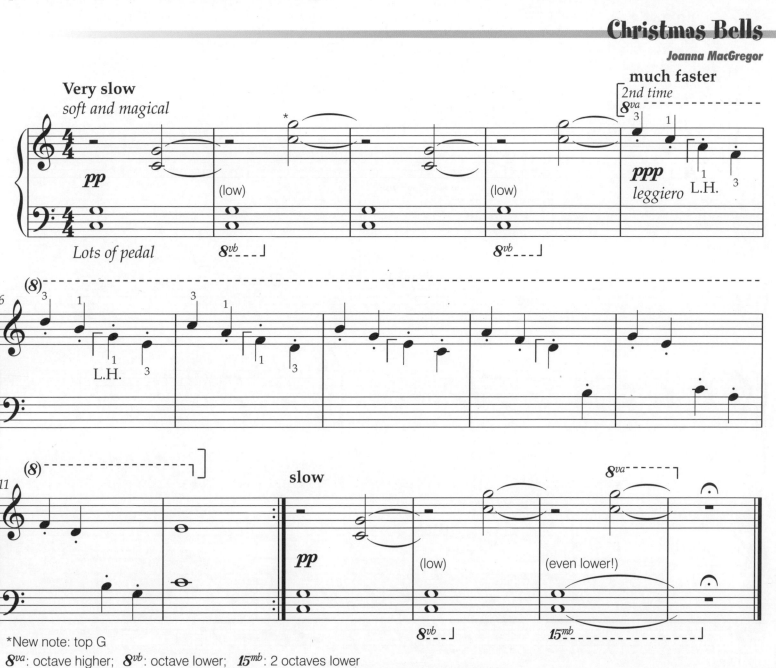

*New note: top G

8va: octave higher; 8vb: octave lower; 15^{mb}: 2 octaves lower

Back at home, Ned sat by the fire, wrapped in a blanket and eating mince pies. He was surrounded by his friends, who hugged and kissed him. 'Don't ever leave us again!' they cried. Grumper wiped a small tear from his eye. 'I suppose Christmas isn't so bad, after all' he admitted, and shouted 'Happy Christmas, PianoWorld!'

We wish you a merry Christmas

Este's Psalter (1592)

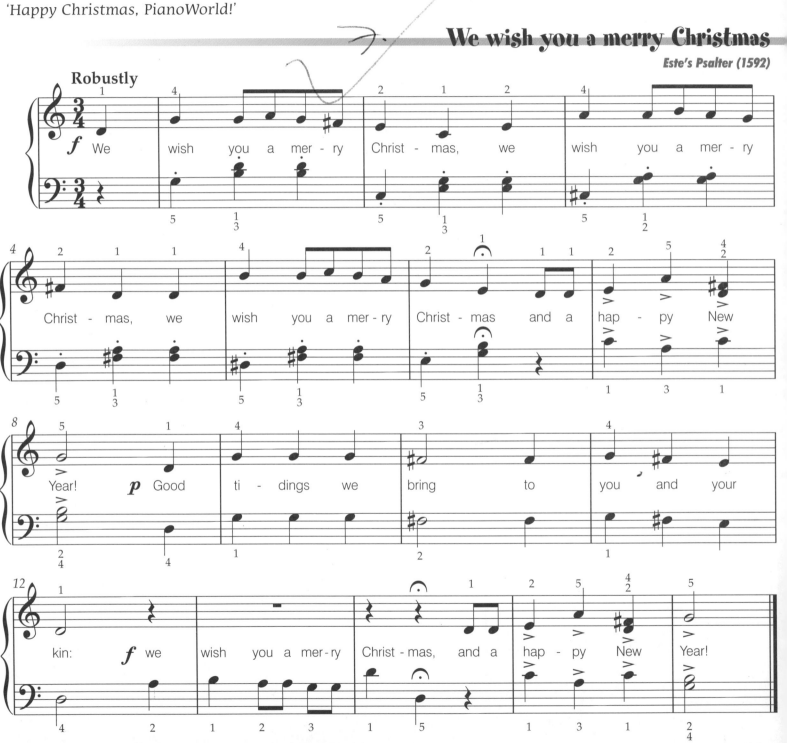